Edward Cline

A HANDBOOK ON ISLAM

A Counter-Jihad Guide for the Uninitiated, the Ill-Advised, the Misinformed, and the Lied-To

Patrick Henry Press

Library of Congress Cataloguing-in-Publication Data

Edward Cline (1946 -)
A Handbook on Islam: A Counter-Jihad Guide for the Uninitiated, the Ill-Advised, the Misinformed, and the Lied-To

ISBN-13: 978-1512315318
ISBN-10: 1512315311
ASIN: B00Y14ZZU6

The Patrick Henry Press
Williamsburg, VA

Publisher's Note: The author and The Patrick Henry Press have made every effort to ensure the accuracy of the information contained herein.

Table of Contents

Preface by the Author

A Handbook on Islam is intended to be a supplementary guide to *Islam's Reign of Terror*, which was published by the Voltaire Press in 2013. The latter title offers a chronicle of terrorist acts committed since 9/11, which, as of the date of this writing, have neared 26,000 separate and deadly attacks of varying magnitudes. These attacks are now commonplace and are occurring daily, chiefly in the Mideast and in Africa, committed by ISIS (or 'ISIL," or the "Islamic State"), which has established beachheads in Libya and in Nigeria and in other unstable countries in that region. "Outbreaks" of Islamic terrorism – or Islamic mob rule – are occurring in the Far East in Pakistan and Afghanistan, when Islamic fundamentalists not necessarily connected with ISIS or Al-Qaeda persecute or slaughter Christians or target individuals for execution.

Attacks continue in Europe and in the U.S., ostensively in "retaliation" for drawing images of Mohammad, the alleged prophet of Islam. In early January 7th 2015 Saïd and Chérif Kouachi, forced their way into the Paris offices of Charlie Hebdo, the French weekly satirical newspaper, and killed eleven of the staff, and later killed a French police officer who was directing traffic. Following that, more attacks occurred in other regions of France. In the U.S., Pamela Geller's Draw Mohammad contest and event in Garland, Texas, on May 3rd 2015 was attacked by two Muslim "extremists" armed with automatic weapons; the gunmen made it only as far as the building's parking lot before being shot dead by a single policeman.

And, more than a supplementary guide, the author thought it a necessary work to help counteract the mainstream media's refusal, inability, or unwillingness to grasp the perilous seriousness of the ends and means of Islamic terrorism and terrorist acts committed in the U.S. and abroad. The handicap under which the MSM acts and speaks is a professed but qualified adherence to the First Amendment of the U.S. Constitution and an professed reverence for the freedom of speech, coupled with a condemnation of anyone or any event that defies the Islamic Sharia prohibition against drawing or depicting Mohammad in any manner for any reason. Pamela Geller was viciously attacked by most television political critics and in most newspapers for openly and specifically flouting the Sharia prohibition by holding the contest and the event, and was accused of "baiting" Muslim terrorists. Her allegedly ulterior motives came under fire, but not those of the terrorists, which were openly homicidal and no secret to the federal government, to the MSM, or to the intended victims.

The Mohammad cartoon by Bosch Fawstin that won
Pamela Geller's Draw Mohammad contest in Garland, Texas

One wonders how Geller's vitriolic critics and character assassins – including business tycoon and Islam-friendly Donald Trump – would have responded to the Boston Tea Party, when Americans openly defied Crown mercantile rule by boarding a British merchant vessel and dumping its tea cargo into Boston Harbor. Would they have deemed it "baiting" the British, or a form of "irresponsible speech," or an instance of "Anglophobic entrapment"? Too likely, given the record of craven verisimilitude of our news anchors and politicians, who are the true "Islamophobes," else why are they so frightened of discussing Islam? Too likely, also, they would argue that banks exist so that they can entrap bank robbers.

In Great Britain, in Europe, and in the Middle and Far East, it is now codified law that any speech against or criticism of any aspect of Islam by a non-Muslim is designated a punishable offense. However, a state of *dhimmitude,* that is, of submission to Islam, in especially the U.K. and Continental Europe, allows Muslim clerics and Muslim street demonstrators to excoriate other faiths and demand that Sharia law be imposed across the board in countries to which large numbers of Muslims have "immigrated" or "settled" – or, as some Western critics and observers have characterized it, "invaded," a term which better comports with the Muslim Brotherhood strategy of "civilizational jihad."

There are over 2,100 mosques in the U.S., and the number is growing, thanks to Obama's policy of admitting Muslims from the four corners of Islam. Many American mosques preach violent or subtle jihad against America and Americans. Many of the convicted domestic jihadists come from American mosques. Boston Marathon bomber Dzhokhar Tsarnaev and his brother attended a Boston-area mosque that preached jihad. Nadir Soofi and Elton Simpson, the Garland, Texas, the two dead gunmen who attempted to attack the Draw Mohammad event, attended the same Phoenix, Arizona mosque.

More vigorous action against Muslim rape gangs in Britain and attacks on non-Muslim women on the Continent is not forthcoming because authorities fear the charge of "racism" and "bigotry," even though the overall victim profile reflects a motivational and doctrinal racism on the part of Muslim perpetrators. Anti-Semitism is on the rise in Europe, led by Islamic clerics and other Muslim proselytizers, and in the U.S., spearheaded by leftists who find Islamic anti-Semitism copasetic with their own political designs on Israel and Jews.

ISIS has boasted that it has planted agents of terrorism in the U.S. and that it has established training camps for terrorists across the border in Mexico. Our government has documented these facts, especially the one that many terrorists are infiltrating into the country over the "open" border in the guise of illegal immigrants.

These are in addition to the terrorist "sleeper cells" established by Hamas. From *Islam's Reign of Terror*:

Hamas has sleeper cells in the U.S., one of which awoke to execute the Boston Marathon bombings of April 15th....

Terrorist sleeper cells are located primarily in Virginia, New York, North Carolina, Michigan, Florida, California, and Canada. The "sleepers" are prepared to conduct terrorist attacks within the U.S., and nuclear material is available to them. "Prepared" in this instance indicates they have the necessary tools to carry out their attacks and are prepared to die....

Terrorist operations are active in the U.S. and are being operated/financed by Al-Qaeda throughout the U.S. [pp. 25-27]

Political correctness, ubiquitous moral turpitude, and an intellectual disorder – or what one could call the "British cerebral palsy" syndrome, or a fear of being called "racist" – stops the MSM and our politicians from discussing these issues or challenging President Barack Obama on his openly pro-Islam policies and his open-border policy of allowing uncountable illegal immigrants to settle in the U.S. to comprise a fresh voting bloc for the Democrats and Progressives.

In too many instances, the MSM and our political leaders have voluntarily adopted the mental headdress of *dhimmitude* in their policies *vis-à-vis* Islam and terrorism. Islamic terrorists are referred to in speeches and editorials as "extremists," "radicals," "lone wolves," and "rogue" Muslims who have "hijacked" a "peaceful" religion, ignorant of or not caring to recognize that the murder and mayhem committed by Muslims – whether or not these individuals were born into the religion, or were converts to it – are consistent with the dozens of violent verses to be found in the *Koran* and the *Hadith*.

These verses are the main feature of the *Handbook*, together with a Lexicon of Islamic/Arabic terms and some material from *Islam's Reign of Terror*.

It is important that non-Muslim citizens understand the forces that have been launched against them and that they educate themselves on the means and ends of those forces. By and large, their "protectors" in the federal and civil government realms have abandoned them in favor of political correctness when the issues are Islam and Muslim immigration to the U.S. and the West. It is hoped that the *Handbook*, together with *Islam's Reign of Terror*, will help them understand the nature of their enemies, in Islam and in our own governments.

The Violent Koranic Verses

By way of an introduction to the violent Koranic verses, here is what American author and neuroscientist Sam Harris has written about the violence inherent in Islam. Punctuation and style are in the original as published by Religion of Peace and Answering Islam.

Open the Koran, which is perfect in its every syllable, and simply read it with the eyes of faith. You will see how little compassion need be wasted on those whom God himself is in the process of "mocking," "cursing," "shaming," "punishing," "scourging," "judging," "burning," "annihilating," "not forgiving," and "not reprieving." God, who is infinitely wise, has cursed the infidels with their doubts. He prolongs their life and prosperity so that they may continue heaping sin upon sin and all the more richly deserve the torments that await them beyond the grave. In this light, the people who died on Sept. 11 were nothing more than fuel for the eternal fires of God's justice.

To convey the relentlessness with which unbelievers are vilified in the text of the Koran, I provide a long compilation of quotations below, in order of their appearance in the text. This is what the Creator of the universe apparently has on his mind (when he is not fussing with gravitational constants and atomic weights).

Qur'an :2:191-193: "And slay them wherever you come upon them, and expel them from where they expelled you; persecution is more grievous than slaying. But fight them not by the Holy Mosque until they should fight you there; then, if they fight you, slay them — such is the recompense of unbelievers, but if they give over, surely Allah is All-forgiving, All-compassionate. Fight them, till there is no persecution and the religion is Allah's; then if they give over, there shall be no enmity save for evildoers."

Qur'an 4:34: "Men are the managers of the affairs of women for that Allah has preferred in bounty one of them over another, and for that they have expended of their property. Righteous women are therefore obedient, guarding the secret for Allah's guarding. And those you fear may be rebellious admonish; banish them to their couches, and beat them. If they then obey you, look not for any way against them; Allah is All-high, All-great."

Qur'an 4:89: "They wish that you should disbelieve as they disbelieve, and then you would be equal; therefore take not to yourselves friends of them, until they emigrate in the way of Allah; then, if they turn their backs, take them, and slay them wherever you find them; take not to yourselves any one of them as friend or helper."

Qur'an 5:33: "This is the recompense of those who fight against Allah and His Messenger, and hasten about the earth, to do corruption there: they shall be slaughtered, or crucified, or their hands and feet shall alternately be struck off; or they shall be banished from the land. That is a degradation for them in this world; and in the world to come awaits them a mighty chastisement."

Qur'an 5:38: "And the thief, male and female: cut off the hands of both, as a recompense for what they have earned, and a punishment exemplary from Allah; Allah is All-mighty, All-wise."

Qur'an 8:12: "When thy Lord was revealing to the angels, 'I am with you; so confirm the believers. I shall cast into the unbelievers' hearts terror; so smite above the necks, and smite every finger of them!'"

Qur'an 8:39: "Fight them, till there is no persecution and the religion is Allah's entirely; then if they give over, surely Allah sees the things they do."

Qur'an 8:60: "Make ready for them whatever force and strings of horses you can, to terrify thereby the enemy of Allah and your enemy, and others besides them that you know not; Allah knows them. And

7

whatsoever you expend in the way of Allah shall be repaid you in full; you will not be wronged."

Qur'an 9:5: "Then, when the sacred months are drawn away, slay the idolaters wherever you find them, and take them, and confine them, and lie in wait for them at every place of ambush. But if they repent, and perform the prayer, and pay the alms, then let them go their way; Allah is All-forgiving, All-compassionate."

Qur'an 9:29: "Fight those who believe not in Allah and the Last Day and do not forbid what Allah and His Messenger have forbidden — such men as practise not the religion of truth, being of those who have been given the Book — until they pay the tribute out of hand and have been humbled."

Qur'an 9:111: "Allah has bought from the believers their selves and their possessions against the gift of Paradise; they fight in the way of Allah; they kill, and are killed; that is a promise binding upon Allah in the Torah, and the Gospel, and the Koran; and who fulfils his covenant truer than Allah? So rejoice in the bargain you have made with Him; that is the mighty triumph."

Qur'an 9:123: "O believers, fight the unbelievers who are near to you; and let them find in you a harshness; and know that Allah is with the god-fearing."

Qur'an 47:4: "When you meet the unbelievers, smite their necks, then, when you have made wide slaughter among them, tie fast the bonds; then set them free, either by grace or ransom, till the war lays down its loads. So it shall be; and if Allah had willed, He would have avenged Himself upon them; but that He may try some of you by means of others. And those who are slain in the way of Allah, He will not send their works astray."

Qur'an 5:3 This day have I perfected your religion for you and completed My favor upon you and have chosen for you Islam as your religion.

Qur'an 54:17 And We have indeed made the Qur'an easy to understand and remember, then is there any that will remember (or receive admonition)?

Qur'an 9:88 The Messenger and those who believe with him, strive hard and fight with their wealth and lives in Allah's Cause.

Qur'an 9:5 Fight and kill the disbelievers wherever you find them, take them captive, harass them, lie in wait and ambush them using every stratagem of war.

Qur'an 9:112 The Believers fight in Allah's Cause, they slay and are slain, kill and are killed.

Qur'an 9:29 Fight those who do not believe until they all surrender, paying the protective tax in submission.

Ishaq 325 "Muslims, fight in Allah's Cause. Stand firm and you will prosper. Help the Prophet, obey him, give him your allegiance, and your religion will be victorious."

Qur'an 8:39 "Fight them until all opposition ends and all submit to Allah."

Qur'an 8:39 "So fight them until there is no more Fitnah (disbelief [non-Muslims]) and all submit to the religion of Allah alone (in the whole world)."

Ishaq 324 "He said, 'Fight them so that there is no more rebellion, and religion, all of it, is for Allah only. Allah must have no rivals.'"

Qur'an 9:14 "Fight them and Allah will punish them by your hands, lay them low, and cover them with shame. He will help you over them."

Ishaq 300 "I am fighting in Allah's service. This is piety and a good deed. In Allah's war I do not fear as others should. For this fighting is righteous, true, and good."

Ishaq 587 "Our onslaught will not be a weak faltering affair. We shall fight as long as we live. We will fight until you turn to Islam, humbly seeking refuge. We will fight not caring whom we meet. We will fight whether we destroy ancient holdings or newly gotten gains. We have mutilated every opponent. We have driven them violently before us at the command of Allah and Islam. We will fight until our religion is established. And we will plunder them, for they must suffer disgrace."

Qur'an 8:65 "O Prophet, urge the faithful to fight. If there are twenty among you with determination they will vanquish two hundred; if there are a hundred then they will slaughter a thousand unbelievers, for the infidels are a people devoid of understanding."

Ishaq 326 "Prophet exhort the believers to fight. If there are twenty good fighters they will defeat two hundred for they are a senseless people. They do not fight with good intentions nor for truth."

Hadith, Sahih Bukhari V4B52N63 "A man whose face was covered with an iron mask came to the Prophet and said, 'Allah's Apostle! Shall I fight or embrace Islam first?' The Prophet said, 'Embrace Islam first and then fight.' So he embraced Islam, and was martyred. Allah's Apostle said, 'A Little work, but a great reward.'"

Hadith, Bukhari V4B53N386 "Our Prophet, the Messenger of our Lord, ordered us to fight you till you worship Allah alone or pay us the Jizyah tribute tax in submission. Our Prophet has informed us that our Lord says: 'Whoever amongst us is killed as a martyr shall go to Paradise to lead such a luxurious life as he has never seen, and whoever survives shall become your master.'"

Hadith, Sahih Muslim C34B20N4668 "The Messenger said: 'Anybody who equips a warrior going to fight in the Way of Allah is like one who actually fights. And anybody who looks after his family in his absence is also like one who actually fights."

Qur'an 9:38 "Believers, what is the matter with you, that when you are asked to go forth and fight in Allah's Cause you cling to the earth? Do you prefer the life of this world to the Hereafter? Unless you go forth,

He will afflict and punish you with a painful doom, and put others in your place."

Qur'an 9:123 "Fight the unbelievers around you, and let them find harshness in you."

Qur'an 8:72 "Those who accepted Islam and left their homes to fight in Allah's Cause with their possessions and persons, and those who gave (them) asylum, aid, and shelter, those who harbored them – these are allies of one another. You are not responsible for protecting those who embraced Islam but did not leave their homes [to fight] until they do so." [Another translation reads:] "You are only called to protect Muslims who fight."

Hadith, Sahih Muslim C9B1N31 "I have been commanded to fight against people till they testify to the fact that there is no god but Allah, and believe in me (that) I am the Messenger and in all that I have brought."

Hadith, Bukhari V9B84N59 "Whoever says this will save his property and life from me."

Qur'an 8:73 "The unbelieving infidels are allies. Unless you (Muslims) aid each other (fighting as one united block to make Allah's religion victorious), there will be confusion and mischief. Those who accepted Islam, left their homes to fight in Allah's Cause (al-Jihad), as well as those who give them asylum, shelter, and aid – these are (all) Believers: for them is pardon and bountiful provision (in Paradise)."

Tabari IX:69 "Arabs are the most noble people in lineage, the most prominent, and the best in deeds. We were the first to respond to the call of the Prophet. We are Allah's helpers and the viziers of His Messenger. We fight people until they believe in Allah. He who believes in Allah and His Messenger has protected his life and possessions from us. As for one who disbelieves, we will fight him forever in the Cause of Allah. Killing him is a small matter to us."

Qur'an 48:16 "Say (Muhammad) to the wandering desert Arabs who lagged behind: 'You shall be invited to fight against a people given to war with mighty prowess. You shall fight them until they surrender and submit. If you obey, Allah will grant you a reward, but if you turn back, as you did before, He will punish you with a grievous torture."

Qur'an 48:22 "If the unbelieving infidels fight against you, they will retreat. (Such has been) the practice (approved) of Allah in the past: no change will you find in the ways of Allah."

Qur'an 47:4 "When you clash with the unbelieving Infidels in battle (fighting Jihad in Allah's Cause), smite their necks until you overpower them, killing and wounding many of them. At length, when you have thoroughly subdued them, bind them firmly, making (them) captives. Thereafter either generosity or ransom (them based upon what benefits Islam) until the war lays down its burdens. Thus are you commanded by Allah to continue carrying out Jihad against the unbelieving infidels until they submit to Islam."

Qur'an 47:31 "And We shall try you until We know those among you who are the fighters."

Tabari VI:138 "Those present at the oath of Aqabah had sworn an allegiance to Muhammad. It was a pledge of war against all men. Allah had permitted fighting."

Tabari VI:139 "Allah had given his Messenger permission to fight by revealing the verse 'And fight them until persecution is no more, and religion is all for Allah.'"

Qur'an 9:19 "Do you make the giving of drink to pilgrims, or the maintenance of the Mosque, equal to those who fight in the Cause of Allah? They are not comparable in the sight of Allah. Those who believe, and left their homes, striving with might, fighting in Allah's Cause with their goods and their lives, have the highest rank in the sight of Allah."

Ishaq 550 "The Muslims met them with their swords. They cut through many arms and skulls. Only confused cries and groans could be heard over our battle roars and snarling."

Qur'an 5:94 "Believers, Allah will make a test for you in the form of a little game in which you reach out for your lances. Any who fails this test will have a grievous punishment."

Ishaq 578 "Crushing the heads of the infidels and splitting their skulls with sharp swords, we continually thrust and cut at the enemy. Blood gushed from their deep wounds as the battle wore them down. We conquered bearing the Prophet's fluttering war banner. Our cavalry was submerged in rising dust, and our spears quivered, but by us the Prophet gained victory."

Tabari IX:22 "The Prophet continued to besiege the town, fighting them bitterly."

Tabari IX:25 "By Allah, I did not come to fight for nothing. I wanted a victory over Ta'if so that I might obtain a slave girl from them and make her pregnant."

Tabari IX:82 "The Messenger sent Khalid with an army of 400 to Harith [a South Arabian tribe] and ordered him to invite them to Islam for three days before he fought them. If they were to respond and submit, he was to teach them the Book of Allah, the Sunnah of His Prophet, and the requirements of Islam. If they should decline, then he was to fight them."

Tabari IX:88 "Abdallah Azdi came to the Messenger, embraced Islam, and became a good Muslim. Allah's Apostle invested Azdi with the authority over those who had surrendered and ordered him to fight the infidels from the tribes of Yemen. Azdi left with an army by the Messenger's command. The Muslims besieged them for a month. Then they withdrew, setting a trap. When the Yemenites went in pursuit, Azdi was able to inflict a heavy loss on them."

Ishaq 530 "Get out of his way, you infidel unbelievers. Every good thing goes with the Apostle. Lord, I believe in his word. We will fight you about its interpretations as we have fought you about its revelation with strokes that will remove heads from shoulders and make enemies of friends."

13

Hadith, Sahih Muslim C9B1N29 "Command For Fighting Against People So Long As They Do Not Profess That There Is No Ilah (God) But Allah And Muhammad Is His Messenger: When the Messenger breathed his last and Bakr was appointed Caliph, many Arabs chose to become apostates [rejected Islam]. Abu Bakr said: 'I will definitely fight against anyone who stops paying the Zakat tax, for it is an obligation. I will fight against them even to secure the cord used for hobbling the feet of a camel which they used to pay if they withhold it now.' Allah had justified fighting against those who refused to pay Zakat."

Hadith, Sahih Muslim C9B1N33 "The Prophet said: 'I have been commanded to fight against people till they testify there is no god but Allah, that Muhammad is the Messenger of Allah, and they establish prostration prayer, and pay Zakat. If they do it, their blood and property are protected.'"

Hadith, Sahih Muslim C10B1N176 "Muhammad (may peace be upon him) sent us in a raiding party. We raided Huraqat in the morning. I caught hold of a man and he said: 'There is no god but Allah,' but I attacked him with a spear anyway. It once occurred to me that I should ask the Apostle about this. The Messenger said: 'Did he profess "There is no god but Allah," and even then you killed him?' I said: 'He made a profession out of the fear of the weapon I was threatening him with.' The Prophet said: 'Did you tear out his heart in order to find out whether it had professed truly or not?'"

Hadith, Sahih Muslim C20B1N4597 "The Prophet said at the conquest of Mecca: 'There is no migration now, but only Jihad, fighting for the Cause of Islam. When you are asked to set out on a Jihad expedition, you should readily do so.'"

Hadith, Sahih Muslim C28B20N4628 "Allah has undertaken to provide for one who leaves his home to fight for His Cause and to affirm the truth of His word; Allah will either admit him to Paradise or will bring him back home with his reward and booty."

Hadith, Sahih Muslim C28B20N4629 "The Messenger said: 'One who is wounded in the Way of Allah – and Allah knows best who is wounded in His Way – will appear on the Day of Judgment with his wound still bleeding. The color (of its discharge) will be blood, (but) its smell will be musk.'"

Hadith, Sahih Muslim C34B20N4652-3 "The Merit Of Jihad And Of Keeping Vigilance Over The Enemy: A man came to the Holy Prophet and said: 'Who is the best of men?' He replied: 'A man who fights staking his life and spending his wealth in Allah's Cause.'"

Hadith, Sahih Muslim C42B20N4684 "A desert Arab came to the Prophet and said: 'Messenger, one man fights for the spoils of war; another fights that he may be remembered, and one fights that he may see his (high) position (achieved as a result of his valor in fighting). Which of these is fighting in the Cause of Allah?' The Messenger of Allah said: 'Who fights so that the word of Allah is exalted is fighting in the Way of Allah.'"

Hadith, Sahih Muslim C53B20N4717 "The Prophet said: 'This religion will continue to exist, and a group of people from the Muslims will continue to fight for its protection until the Hour is established.'"

Hadith, Bukhari V5B59N288 "I witnessed a scene that was dearer to me than anything I had ever seen. Aswad came to the Prophet while Muhammad was urging the Muslims to fight the pagans. He said, 'We shall fight on your right and on your left and in front of you and behind you.' I saw the face of the Prophet getting bright with happiness, for that saying delighted him."

Hadith, Bukhari V5B59N290 "The believers who did not join the Ghazwa [Islamic raid or invasion] and those who fought are not equal in reward."

Qur'an 2:193 "Fight them until there is no more Fitnah (disbelief) and religion is only for Allah. But if they cease/desist, let there be no hostility except against infidel disbelievers."

Qur'an 2:217 "They question you concerning fighting in the sacred month. Say: 'Fighting therein is a grave (matter); but to prevent access to Allah, to deny Him, to prevent access to the Sacred Mosque, to expel its members, and polytheism are worse than slaughter. Nor will they cease fighting you until they make you renegades from your religion. If any of you turn back and die in unbelief, your works will be lost and you will go to Hell. Surely those who believe and leave their homes to fight in Allah's Cause have the hope of Allah's mercy."

Qur'an 2:244 "Fight in Allah's Cause, and know that Allah hears and knows all."

Qur'an 2:246 "He said: 'Would you refrain from fighting if fighting were prescribed for you?' They said: 'How could we refuse to fight in Allah's Cause?'"

Ishaq 280 "The Apostle prepared for war in pursuance of Allah's command to fight his enemies and to fight the infidels who Allah commanded him to fight."

Qur'an 61:2 "O Muslims, why say one thing and do another? Grievously odious and hateful is it in the sight of Allah that you say that which you do not. Truly Allah loves those who fight in His Cause in a battle array, as if they were a solid cemented structure."

Hadith, Bukhari V4B52N61 "Allah's Apostle! We were absent from the first battle you fought against the pagans. If Allah gives us a chance to do battle, no doubt, He will see how bravely we fight."

Ishaq 398 "Ask them for their help. Thereby make the religion of Islam agreeable to them. And when you are resolved in the matter of religion concerning fighting your enemy you will have the advantage."

Qur'an 3:146 "How many prophets fought in Allah's Cause? With them (fought) myriads of godly men who were slain. They never lost heart if they met with disaster in Allah's Cause, nor did they weaken nor give in. Allah loves those who are firm and steadfast [warriors]."

Ishaq 393 "How many prophets has death in battle befallen and how many multitudes with him? They did not show weakness toward their enemies and were not humiliated when they suffered in the fight for

Allah and their religion. That is steadfastness. Allah loves the steadfast."

Qur'an 3:153 "Behold! You ran off precipitately, climbing up the high hill without even casting a side glance at anyone, while the Messenger in your rear is calling you from your rear, urging you to fight. Allah gave you one distress after another by way of requital, to teach you not to grieve for the booty that had escaped you and for (the ill) that had befallen you."

Qur'an 3:154 "Say: 'Even if you had remained in your houses, those ordained to be slaughtered would have gone forth to the places where they were to slain."

Ishaq 440 "Helped by the Holy Spirit we smited Muhammad's foes. The Apostle sent a message to them with a sharp cutting sword."

Ishaq 470 "We attacked them fully armed, swords in hand, cutting through heads and skulls."

Qur'an 61:4 "Surely Allah loves those who fight in His Cause."

Qur'an 61:11 "Believers, shall I lead you to a bargain or trade that will save you from a painful torment? That you believe in Allah and His Messenger (Muhammad), and that you strive and fight in Allah's Cause with your property and your lives: That will be best for you!" Qur'an 61:12 "He will forgive you your sins, and admit you to Gardens under which rivers flow, and to beautiful mansions in Eden: that is indeed the Supreme Achievement. And another (favor) which you love: help from Allah for a speedy victory over your enemies."

Qur'an 8:5 "Your Lord ordered you out of your homes to fight for the true cause, even though some Muslims disliked it, and were averse (to fighting)."

Qur'an 24:53 "They swear their strongest oaths saying that if only you would command them. They would leave their homes (and go forth fighting in Allah's Cause). Say: 'Swear not; Obedience is (more) reasonable.'"

Qur'an 4:74 "Let those who fight in Allah's Cause sell this world's life for the hereafter. To him who fights in Allah's Cause, whether he is slain or victorious, We shall give him a reward."

Qur'an 4:75 "What reason have you that you should not fight in Allah's Cause?" [Another translation says:] "What is wrong with you that you do not fight for Allah?"

Qur'an 4:76 "Those who believe fight in the Cause of Allah."

Qur'an 4:77 "Have you not seen those to whom it was said: Withhold from fighting, perform the prayer and pay the zakat. But when orders for fighting were issued, a party of them feared men as they ought to have feared Allah. They say: 'Our Lord, why have You ordained fighting for us, why have You made war compulsory?'"

Qur'an 4:78 "Wherever you are, death will find you, even if you are in towers strong and high! So what is wrong with these people, that they fail to understand these simple words?"

Qur'an 4:84 "Then fight (Muhammad) in Allah's Cause. Incite the believers to fight with you."

Qur'an 4:94 "Believers, when you go abroad to fight wars in Allah's Cause, investigate carefully, and say not to anyone who greets you: 'You are not a believer!' Coveting the chance profits of this life (so that you may despoil him). With Allah are plenteous spoils and booty."

Qur'an 4:95 "Not equal are believers who sit home and receive no hurt and those who fight in Allah's Cause with their wealth and lives. Allah has granted a grade higher to those who fight with their possessions and bodies to those who sit home. Those who fight He has distinguished with a special reward." (An extra bag of pork rinds?)

Qur'an 4:100 "He who leaves his home in Allah's Cause finds abundant resources and many a refuge. Should he die as a refugee for Allah and His Messenger His reward becomes due and sure with Allah. When you travel through the earth there is no blame on you if you curtail your worship for fear unbelievers may attack you. In truth the disbelievers are your enemy."

Qur'an 4:102 "When you (Prophet) lead them in prayer, let some stand with you, taking their arms with them. When they finish their prostrations, let them take positions in the rear. And let others who have not yet prayed come – taking all precaution, and bearing arms. The Infidels wish, if you were negligent of your arms, to assault you in a rush. But there is no blame on you if you put away your arms because of the inconvenience of rain or because you are ill; but take precaution. For the Unbelieving Infidels Allah hath prepared a humiliating punishment."

Qur'an 4:2:191-193: "And slay them wherever you come upon them, and expel them from where they expelled you; persecution is more grievous than slaying. But fight them not by the Holy Mosque until they should fight you there; then, if they fight you, slay them — such is the recompense of unbelievers, but if they give over, surely Allah is All-forgiving, All-compassionate. Fight them, till there is no persecution and the religion is Allah's; then if they give over, there shall be no enmity save for evildoers."

Qur'an 4:4:34: "Men are the managers of the affairs of women for that Allah has preferred in bounty one of them over another, and for that they have expended of their property. Righteous women are therefore obedient, guarding the secret for Allah's guarding. And those you fear may be rebellious admonish; banish them to their couches, and beat them. If they then obey you, look not for any way against them; Allah is All-high, All-great."

Qur'an 4:4:89: "They wish that you should disbelieve as they disbelieve, and then you would be equal; therefore take not to yourselves friends of them, until they emigrate in the way of Allah; then, if they turn their backs, take them, and slay them wherever you find them; take not to yourselves any one of them as friend or helper."

Qur'an 4:5:33: "This is the recompense of those who fight against Allah and His Messenger, and hasten about the earth, to do corruption there: they shall be slaughtered, or crucified, or their hands and feet shall alternately be struck off; or they shall be banished from the land. That is a degradation for them in this world; and in the world to come awaits them a mighty chastisement."

Qur'an 4:5:38: "And the thief, male and female: cut off the hands of both, as a recompense for what they have earned, and a punishment exemplary from Allah; Allah is All-mighty, All-wise."

Qur'an 4:8:12: "When thy Lord was revealing to the angels, 'I am with you; so confirm the believers. I shall cast into the unbelievers' hearts terror; so smite above the necks, and smite every finger of them!'"

Qur'an 4:8:39: "Fight them, till there is no persecution and the religion is Allah's entirely; then if they give over, surely Allah sees the things they do."

Qur'an 4:8:60: "Make ready for them whatever force and strings of horses you can, to terrify thereby the enemy of Allah and your enemy, and others besides them that you know not; Allah knows them. And whatsoever you expend in the way of Allah shall be repaid you in full; you will not be wronged."

Qur'an 4:9:5: "Then, when the sacred months are drawn away, slay the idolaters wherever you find them, and take them, and confine them, and lie in wait for them at every place of ambush. But if they repent, and perform the prayer, and pay the alms, then let them go their way; Allah is All-forgiving, All-compassionate."

Qur'an 4:9:29: "Fight those who believe not in Allah and the Last Day and do not forbid what Allah and His Messenger have forbidden — such men as practice not the religion of truth, being of those who have been given the Book — until they pay the tribute out of hand and have been humbled."

Qur'an 4:9:111: "Allah has bought from the believers their selves and their possessions against the gift of Paradise; they fight in the way of Allah; they kill, and are killed; that is a promise binding upon Allah in the Torah, and the Gospel, and the Koran; and who fulfils his covenant truer than Allah? So rejoice in the bargain you have made with Him; that is the mighty triumph."

Qur'an 4:9:123: "O believers, fight the unbelievers who are near to you; and let them find in you a harshness; and know that Allah is with the god-fearing."

Notes:

Muḥammad ibn Isḥāq ibn Yasār ibn Khiyār (704-770 AD)was an Arab Muslim historian and hagiographer who collected oral traditions that formed the basis of an important biography of Mohammad.

Sahih al-Bukhari: According to Bukhari. Bukhari was a Muslim (8th-9th century AD) translator and interpreter who compared Koranic and Hadith texts.

Abu Ja'far Muhammad ibn Jarir al-Tabari (839–923 AD) was a prominent and influential Persian scholar, historian and exegete of the Koran.

Sources: The Religion of Peace at:
http://www.thereligionofpeace.com/Quran/023-violence.htm
Answering Islam at:
http://www.answering-islam.org/Quran/Themes/jihad_passages.html
Sam Harris quotation:
https://thegreatone22.wordpress.com/2013/05/19/sam-harris-verses-from-the-koran/

This is an excerpt from *Islam's Reign of Terror* on the cultural genesis of Islam. It helps to explain why such a primitive, alien religion and ideology have taken root in the West, and how leftist ideology, pragmatism, and the leveling power of egalitarianism practically invited Islam to destroy Western culture "from within."

THE CULTURAL ROOTS OF TERRORISM

The cancerous progress of Islam in the West is made possible by, among other modern "isms," multiculturalism and egalitarianism.

Egalitarianism seeks "equality of results." Outcomes and results must be equal for all, whether the value is wealth, fame, honors, or admission to prestigious colleges. In pushing redistribution schemes, egalitarians regard as irrelevant one's talent, intelligence, effort, virtue. To rectify the so-called unfairness of some individuals being more talented or more able than others, egalitarians tell us that we must hobble, raze, and ridicule the best. We must "comfort the afflicted, and afflict the comfortable." We must give our heroes feet of clay. We must sacrifice the best to the worst.

In practice, egalitarianism means that a criminal empire is to be admired as much as Steve Jobs' computer empire, that we must have scoreless soccer games to bolster the feelings of less talented players, that beauty contests "disadvantage" the ugly, that the healthy make the obese feel bad.

Egalitarianism demands non-judgmental acceptance of everyone's opinions. (There is no absolute truth, the purveyors of egalitarianism say, and no knowable reality in which to find it.) Since no opinion or value judgment is more valid than any another, egalitarianism reduces all such judgments to the lowest common denominator. On this view, Aristotle's gift of reason to Western civilization, the Renaissance his philosophy spawned, and the science-loving Enlightenment that improved man's life – all of this is to be immolated to the death-worshipping creed of Islam.

Multiculturalism is egalitarianism applied to cultures. It proclaims that no culture is superior to another. In practice, the only way to achieve such equality of results among cultures is to tear down the best, i.e., the West. To achieve equality between the great and the depraved, we must, claim multiculturalists, surrender to Islamic terror and tyranny our freedoms and wealth. After all, say multiculturalists, who are we to claim that it's better to use an airplane for travel than it is to use one for mass murder?

The disease of multiculturalism spreads like this. First it blurs all cultural distinctions, i.e., it performs a kind of value lobotomy on the minds in the West. Then any second-rate, third-rate, or nihilistic cultural "values" rush in to fill the void. One sees examples of this in the demands that the Ground Zero mosque be afforded the same respect as the Iwo Jima monument in Washington D.C., or in the calls for the use of Sharia law instead of Western jurisprudence.

The Western mind used to value Patrick Henry's "give me liberty or give me death," the *Bill of Rights*, and the *Declaration of Independence*. But those "cultural prejudices" are being wiped clean by multiculturalism. And now, the West's values are being sacrificed to the lowest and worst culture on earth – an Islamic culture that today demands submission to its reign of terror.

But, philosophically and morally, Islam is an ideology of *nihilism*.

What is nihilism? Briefly, according to *The Merriam-Webster Dictionary*, its philosophical meaning is "a doctrine that denies any objective ground of truth and especially of moral truths." Its political meaning is "a doctrine or belief that conditions in the social organization are so bad as to make destruction desirable for its own sake *independent of any constructive program or possibility*." (*Italics* mine) This means that values as such are candidates for destruction for destruction's sake.[46.]

In Islam, no values may be held outside its prescribed values, and *all* its values are anti-reason, inherently irrational, anti-man, and, fundamentally anti-life. Islamic "values" purportedly are handed down to men by a deity who commands obedience; "Do as I say, because I say so." All other values, *including* one's life, are of no consequence and may be eliminated or destroyed *because* they are non-Islamic and conflict with the whole psychology and ideology of submission to the arbitrary diktats of an unknowable being. Islam, in essence, is a creed of living death.

While Islam's brand of nihilism predates by millennia the formulation of the concept of nihilism, one philosopher in particular is responsible for its spread in the West and for the concomitant acceptance in the West of Islam as just another benign religion to which violent "extremists" have given a "bad name." That philosopher is Immanuel Kant. The term *nihilism*, however, was coined by his 18th century contemporary, German Idealist Friedrich Heinrich Jacobi, who, in his own revolt against the Enlightenment, denied the possibility of objective grounds of knowledge, and claimed that "truth" can only be known through *feeling* and *faith*. Like Kant, he devised a system of "reason" in the name of "revelation" by denying the validity of reason.

Kant's philosophical system is much more elaborate and better known. His major works are efforts to defend religion from Enlightenment ideas and influences. To achieve that, he claimed that reality is unknowable, and that reason is the barrier to ultimate truth.[47]

Kant's system of ethics paves the way for Islam's moral code. Central to his ethics is the notion that one has a duty, an unchosen obligation, to sacrifice one's personal inclinations and desires. If one is motivated by personal gain, then one gets no moral credit. The desire for happiness here on earth, claims Kant, is the most evil of all. On this view, the purpose of life is self-abnegation, pain, and suffering. The destruction of values *because* they are values is the essence of nihilism. And in theory and practice, that is Islam.

The next time you read about Islamic suicide bombers and attacks on Americans or Westerners here or abroad, or watch on TV mobs of maniacal Muslims shouting death to America and to hell with freedom of speech, you are witnessing not so much Muslims obeying Mohammad's commands, as seeing Kant's philosophically selfless progeny at work.

To destroy man's desire for happiness and values, one must first destroy reason. Gary Hull, publisher of Voltaire Press, raised an important issue about how Islam is impervious to reason.

"One philosophic key to why, by its nature, Islam is more violent today, and even fascist, than are Christianity and Judaism, is that Islam was never defanged by the Renaissance or the Enlightenment. It was never dragged, kicking and screaming, in acknowledgement of the key political idea of the separation of religion and state. When Ethan Allen, who, like many of the Founders, was a Deist, penned his pamphlet, *Reason: The Only Oracle of Man*, that idea never reached the Islamic world."[48]

And if, perchance, some sultan, caliph, imam or mullah had heard of the idea, it must have been promptly rejected. Reason is antithetical to religious and secular tyrants.

Further, Islam is *anti-intellectual.* Its key documents, the *Koran*, the *Hadith*, and the *Sira*, must be learned by rote memorization. There is no system in them, no underlying logic to their contents. By comparison, much of Christianity and Judaism (because of the influences of ancient Greece and, later, the Renaissance) use elements of Aristotelian logic to reach their conclusions, and to proselytize for their ideologies. But most of the statements in the *Koran* are mere assertions reputedly uttered by Mohammad; in the *Hadith* and *Sira*, instructional anecdotes and homilies of his and his cohorts' barbarity. There are no moral principles that govern Islam, other than to resort to force against men who resist conversion to it or submission as serfs, slaves, or *dhimmis.*

"Moderate" Muslims protest that the *Koran* can be read so that benign moral tenets can be construed and abided by. But because the *Koran* is a permanent declaration of war against man's happiness and reason, there is no way any of its belligerent statements can be "interpreted" to mean anything other than what they say.[49] For example:

Koran 9:5 – Fight and kill the disbelievers wherever you find them, take them captive, harass them, lie in wait and ambush them using every stratagem of war.

Koran 9:112 – The Believers fight in Allah's Cause, they slay and are slain, kill and are killed.

Koran 9:29 – Fight those who do not believe until they all surrender, paying the protective tax [*jizya*] in submission.

Koran 8:39 – So fight them until there is no more *Fitna* and all submit to the religion of Allah alone (in the whole world).

Muḥammad ibn Isḥāq ibn Yasār ibn Khiyār was an 8th century Muslim hagiographer and historian, one of many such collectors of the oral traditions of Islam for the *Sira*. Here are a handful of his "interpretations" of Islam:

Isḥāq 324 – "He said, 'Fight them so that there is no more rebellion, and religion, all of it, is for Allah only. Allah must have no rivals.'"

Isḥāq 440 – "Helped by the Holy Spirit we smote Muhammad's foes. The Apostle sent a message to them with a sharp cutting sword."

Isḥāq 470 – "We attacked them fully armed, swords in hand, cutting through heads and skulls."

"Moderate" Muslims cannot rationally defend Islam. Islam can only be repudiated, root, branch, and tree. Only reason and a this-worldly philosophy can attempt accomplish that goal. And should all the belligerent and anecdotal imperatives be excised from the *Koran* and its companion texts, what would be left would no longer be Islam. There is no more reconciliation possible between reason and the nihilism of Islam than there is between the Bill of Rights and the Mafia code of *Il bacio della morte* ("Kiss of death" bestowed upon a gang's traitor). Islam is incompatible with reason and with life itself.

Source: *Islam's Reign of Terror,* pp. 37-42,

Muslim Raiders in the Past

In a review of a book on Muslim depredations in the name of Islam, a Chapter of ACT! published these observations about the interminable warfare Islam has waged on the West.

In America we normally think of slaves as being Africans. Unfortunately, prior to 1808 Americans were complicit in aiding in the transportation and selling of Africans in this country. This was a shameful, immoral episode in our national history.

But not all slaves were black. Millions of white Christian slaves were taken by Islamic raiders who were following the example of Mohammed. Mohammed is viewed in Islam as the perfect man. His every action is to be emulated by his followers right down to the present day. If Mohammed owned slaves, all of his followers should also own other human beings.

White slaves from Spain, Central and Eastern Europe were shipped to the slave bazaars of the Middle East. Most of the male slaves were castrated to prevent them from marrying female slaves and thus literally severed their line of descent. Most castrated males were used as galley slaves and eunuchs in the vast harems of evil Muslim rulers.

Read the following statistics: In 903 AD when the Christian town of Thessalonica fell to the Muslim hordes over 22,000 Christians were sold into slavery. Again, in 1526 the Turks invaded the Christian country of Hungary. Over 200,000 people were carried into slavery. In 1571 thousands of Greeks living on the island of Cyprus were sent to Istanbul as slaves.

In the 250 year period between 1530 and 1780 over a million Europeans were seized and forced into slavery. Whole coastal towns were depopulated because of these slave raids. Particularly hard hit were the countries of Italy, southern France, Spain and Portugal. The Islamic slaves raiders even preyed on England, Wales and Ireland. Baltimore, Ireland was targeted in 1631. Nearly all of the inhabitants were captured and carried away into the most degrading perpetual enslavement.

Over 7,000 English people were captured between 1622 and 1644. Believe it or not, when the Muslims heard about all the blue-eyed, blonde haired women living in Iceland they began raiding that far off land. Blondes always brought top dollar in the Muslim world's slave markets.

The tragedy is that even today this abhorrent practice still continues. Everywhere strict Muslims live who follow the letter of the Sharia Law you will find a thriving practice of human bondage. Islam is the only world religion that encourages and still practices slavery. If you don't believe me, just ask the Sudanese.

Sources: "When Europeans were slaves: Research Suggests white slavery was much more common than previously believed."
A review of Robert Davis's study, *Christian Slaves, Muslim Masters: White Slavery in the Mediterranean, the Barbary Coast, and Italy, 1500-1800* (Palgrave Macmillan)
. http://researchnews.osu.edu/archive/whtslav.htm
http://researchnews.osu.edu/archive/whtslav.htm
ACT!:
https://actjonesboroar.wordpress.com/2012/10/28/white-european-christian-slaves-taken-by-muslim-raiders/

An Islamic Lexicon

What follows are terms one will not encounter in the standard news story or on broadcast panels whose topic is Islam and terrorism, but they do occasionally turn up on Internet blog sites that feature stories about the latest Islamic horror stories. All of these terms are Anglicized from the Arabic. Many of these terms concern Muslim garb and do not occur in any of the Islamic texts; many do.

Abaya: Muslim cloak with sleeves, usually black with or without decorations, sometimes with a hood

A'bid: A slave, particularly a black slave

Adhan: Islamic call to prayer; in Turkish, **salat**

Ahl al-Dhimmi: The "People of the Book" (all non-Muslims)

Al-Hijra: Islamic conquest through immigration

Al-ʾIkḫwān al-Muslimūn: The Muslim Brotherhood, founded in 1928 in Egypt by Hassan al-Banna to further Islamic expansion in Muslim and non-Muslim worlds

Al-Qaeda: Mohammad's "base" of operations for his jihad, in Medina (c. 622 A.D.)

"Allahuh Akhbar": "God is the greatest"

Akhawat: Muslim "sisters" (in *jihad*)

Amir: Head of an Islamic state; Muslim or tribal leader (variously, Emir)

Ashura: A 10-day Shiite "festival" of the cleansing of the spirit and scourging of the body (self-flagellation with whips or swords to draw blood) in honor of "St." Hussein, grandson of the Prophet

Asra: Prisoners of War

Babouches: Arab sandals

Bayat: Loyalty

Burqa (burka): Woman's garment that covers entire body, except for mesh for eyes

Caliphate: An Islamic state (variously, Khalifah)

Chador: Woman's garment similar to the burqa, but allowing the face to be visible

Chechia: Arab men's head covering
Dar al-Ahd: Camp of (temporary) Truce (with infidel nations)
Dar al-Harb: Muslim enemy land; "Land of War," Camp of War
Dar al-Islam: "Land of Islam", variously, Dar Al-Islam
Dar al-Kufr: Land of unbelief
Dar al-Tabligh: House of Proselytizing
Darura: the Islamic doctrine of "necessity," if Sharia-approved judgments are not possible in Sharia courts, but only in "infidel" courts.
Dawa: Proselytizing; recruitment; money weapon
Deeni: Arabic for "faith"
Dhimmi: Non-Muslim subject living in Dar al-Islam; a vanquished or conquered "protected" person; "bonded one."
Dhimmitude: A state of subjection under Islam
Din: Religion, faith
Djbellah: Loose garment worn by Arab men
Djinn: Desert demon, evil spirit
Dunya: the material world (existence, reality)

Falafel: Fried balls of ground spiced chickpeas and fava beans
Fard: Islamic duty
Fatwa(h): Islamic edict or ruling on any issue, from diet to assassination of apostates
Fsabeelallah: "The Cause of Allah"
Fitna: Strife within a Muslim society, between Muslims
Five Pillars of Wisdom: shahada, haj, sala, zaka, and saum
Fuqaha: Islamic jurisprudence
Ghanimi: Spoils, booty (of war, e.g., women, camels, land, gold, etc.)
Ghazi: "Martyr" (*shaded*); variously, "raiders"
Ghazva: Raid (variously, "razzia")
Gibla: Direction of prayers (Mecca)
Hadd: Islamic punishment
Hadith: The alleged sayings, traditions, anecdotes, teachings, or episodes of Mohammad (or **Sunna**)
Hajah: Muslims woman's headscarf
Hajj, Haj, Hadj: Muslim pilgrimage to Mecca during Ramadan
Haji, Hajji, hadji: One who has made the pilgrimage to Mecca
Halal: Islamic dietary and other rules ("permissible," "allowed," "lawful")

Halifa: Islamic trusteeship over earth
Hanif: Islamic term for pre-Quranic figures who rejected idolatry in favor of monotheism
Haram: Forbidden, not permitted (synonym for harem?)
Harbi: Non-Muslim resident of Dar al-Harb (Camp of War)
Hijab: Woman's hair, chest, and neck covering scarf; variously, hajib
Hijra: Conquest of non-Muslim countries by immigration; also, reference to Mohammad's flight from Mecca to Medina
Hijrah: Muslim pilgrimage
Hisba: Vice police responsible for enforcing female dress codes
Honor Killing: a Sharia-sanctioned murder of a Muslim who has flouted Islamic customs, usually committed by close family members (of a girl or woman)
Hudna: A temporary truce to buy time, regroup for jihad; aka "peace talks"
Hukm: A perpetual death penalty, which does not expire with the death of imam author
Hurriyya: Islamic "freedom," or "perfect slavery" to Allah
Ibram: Ritual purity during pilgrimage to Mecca
ICNA: Islamic Circle of North America
ISNA: Islamic Society of North America
Iddat: A 3-month separation of a married couple (only a man has the right to renew marriage)
Iftar: Prayer time; also a dinner marking end of Ramadan
Ijaz al-Koran: "Miraculous nature of the holy text"
Ijma: Consensus of Islamic scholars (concerning Shariah law)
Ijtihad: Independent thinking or counsel; see al-Ikhawān al-Muslimūn)
Ikhwan: Arabic for "brothers" (in war, in jihad)
Imam: Islamic leader of prayers in mosque ("priest") (Sunni sect of Islam)
Islam: Submission
ISNA: Islamic Society of North America
Izzat: Islamic "honor"
Jahiliyya: Society or culture of "unbelievers"
Jahiliyyah: Society and government of unbelievers, or, pagan ignorance

Jannat firdaus: the highest level of paradise for a religious martyr or *jihadist*

Jihad: Islamic war of conquest (internal or personal "struggle," or belligerence; The Sixth Pillar of Wisdom, so to speak)

Jihadi: Of Jihad, of a belligerent nature in action

Jihadist: Islamic or Muslim warrior

Jibab: Woman's garment leaving only face and hands exposed

Jilbab: Loose-fitting garment worn by Muslim men (much like a nightgown)

Jizya: Special tax on non-Muslims; variously, al-Jeziya

Kaaba (Qaaba): a cube-shaped building in Mecca, Islam's most sacred edifice, containing the silver-encased "Black Stone" (probably a meteorite) and purportedly Abraham's footprint, among other relics. Purportedly dates back to Mohammad's time

Kabin: Soothsayer

Kafir: (kaffir): Unbeliever; infidel

Kameez: Muslim shirt worn with shalwar (var. qameez)

Keffiyah: a checked scarf worn by Muslims (and pseudo-Muslims, usually left-wing sympathizers of Islamic or Muslim causes; resembles a sweat band); inspired by Yasir Arrafat's goofy headgear.

Khalifa: see Amir

Khalifah: Caliphate

Khimar: tent-like robe that covers woman's head, shoulders and chest, with opening for face

Khumua: Mohammad's "take" of loot (1/5th)

Khutba(h): Islamic Friday sermon, delivered by an **iman**

Kilman: Wise man, law-giver (Mohammad)

Kitman: Wisdom

Koran: "Recitation" (of Allah's words via Gabriel to Mohammad)

Khula: A woman who seeks divorce

Kufr: Infidelity; see **kafir**

Madhab: Schools of Islamic jurisprudence

Madrassa: School for studying the **Koran**

Mahram: Male chaperone or guardian for woman in public

MB: Muslim Brotherhood

Milk al-yamin: Sex slaves (captive women)

Minbar: an iman's elevated, canopied pulpit, similar to the Anglican or Episcopalian pulpit

MAS: Muslim American Society

MSA: Muslim Student Association

Mufti: Muslim lawgiver

Mihrab: In a mosque, a semi-circular niche that points to Mecca

Muezzin (muzim): Muslim pseudo- cleric who broadcasts calls to prayer (**adhan**)

Mujabud: A person who "struggles" in Allah's cause

Mujahideen or **Mujaheddin**: Islamic "freedom" fighter

Mullah: Islamic theologian (Shi'ite branch of Islam)

Munafiq: a hypocrite and a secret infidel

Muqallid: one who follows without question or doubt (a Muslim)

Murtadd: Apostate (a convert to another religion)

Mushrikin: Polytheists or pagans

Mutah: "Temporary marriage" to justify rape of "captured" women and prostitution

Mutaween: Religious police (in Saudi Arabia)

Nagas: human "filth" or "unclean ones" (i.e., infidels, Jews), plural

Naji(s): "Unclean ones," or non-Muslims

Nikah: Islamic ceremony for "temporary" marriage; used to justify rape or prostitution**Niqab**: Woman's shroud-like garment that covers the whole head and all her face except for a slit for the eyes; "mask"; usually worn with a black ankle-length abaya or robe**Purdah:** Seclusion of women from the sight of men (involving head or body coverings)**Qadi** or **Qada**: Islamic judge (**Al-Qada** or **Al-Queda**, Islamic "judges")

Qibla(h): The direction Muslims face for prayers, to Mecca

OIC: Organization of Islamic Cooperation (formerly Islamic Conference)

Qitaal: Combat

Rabat: Connection or "bridge"

Ramadan: Islamic month of fasting

Riba: Usary or interest, forbidden by **Koran**

Ridda: Apostasy

Sabi: Women and children prisoners of war

Sahih: Canonical verse from the Hadith

Sala: Prayer five times a day

Salifi: a sect of Islam that advocates violent jihad and strict adherence to Islamic traditions and mores.

Salafist: a Muslim who espouses **Salafism**.

Sauma: month-long fasting during Ramadan (from sun-up to sun-down)

Shahada: Declaration that Allah is only god and Mohammad his prophet (or messenger)

Shahid, shahid: : national Muslim hero; "martyr"

Sahih Sita: Original six Sunna of **Koran**

Shaheel: Islamic martyr

Shalwar: Loose-fitting pants worn by both sexes in Pakistan and Far East

Sharia(h): Islamic law per the **Koran**; "the path"

Shi'ite: An Islamic sect (the Iranian version of Islam)

Shurtat el-adab: Ethics or moral police (or **mutaween**)

Sira: Life of Mohammad

Sunna: Separate teachings of Mohammad (or **Hadith**)

Sunni: An Islamic sect (the Saudi version of Islam)

Surra: Islamic rules of life per Mohammad (singular: sura); also, chapters

Taghut: An idol or false God

Talaq: "I divorce you," said by a Muslim to his wife. End of marriage.

Talib: Islamic student(s); thus **Taliban** (student "force" or "army")

Taqyas: The art of Islamic lying

Taqiyya: Islamic/religious dissimulation, falsehoods, or concealment aimed against non-Muslims, approved by the **Koran** if it advances Islam

Tawriya: Unlimited deceit or lying, including to other Muslims

Ulama: Islamic religious authority; variously, **Ulema**

Umma(h): Global Islamic brotherhood or "community"

Waaqf: Islamic holy dispensation

Wada: To "wash" feet before prayers

Wahhabi: Fundamentalist Islamic doctrine, chiefly Saudi

Wahhabist: Fundamentalist Islamic cleric, principally Saudi

Zakat: An Islamic welfare tax; variation, *zaka*

Zebibah: Black and blue bump on forehead of Muslim from performing prayers, considered a mark of distinction and piety among Muslims
Zina: Sexual immorality, a punishable crime

Note: This Lexicon was compiled by the author. Another glossary or lexicon of Islamic terms can be found at:
http://www.islamfortoday.com/glossary.htm

STATES THAT SPONSOR TERRORISM

What follows is an excerpt from *Islam's Reign of Terror*. Readers might ask: Where do terrorists get the money with which to wage jihad against the West? Who empowers them, and why?

The State Department's National Center for Counter Terrorism lists forty-eight terrorist groups, the majority of them Islamic.[50] But the State Department itself currently lists only four state sponsors of terrorism: Cuba, the Sudan, Iran and Syria.[51] Libya was dropped from the list after the downfall of Omar Qadhaffi, but should be reinstated, for it is now being governed by Muslim Brotherhood and Al Qada proxies. Missing from the State Department list are Saudi Arabia, Pakistan, and Qatar. Egypt, now under the thumb of the Muslim Brotherhood, may in the future qualify as a state that sponsors terrorism.

Other Islamic states that have supported terrorism in the way of transitional locales with the knowledge or support of their governments are Yemen and Somalia. Iraq, "freed" by us from the grip of Saddam Hussein with American lives and treasure, has become a client state of Iran. Indonesia has the highest population of Muslims and also acts as a covert go-between for the funding and coordination of terrorist plots between competing terrorist groups.

Islam as an ideological force is stateless. But states sponsor its actions. Iran is the chief instigator and enabler of Islamic terrorism.

John David Lewis, in his seminal study of warfare, *Nothing Less Than Victory: Decisive Wars and the Lessons of History*, writes that warfare requires of its civilian and military leaders the proper philosophy to defeat an enemy, a philosophy which must include a moral reason. He demonstrates the efficacy of this philosophy by describing the conduct of several wars from the past, from the Greco-Persian Wars between 547 and 446 BC to the American victory over Japan in 1945.

The United States professes to be "at war against terrorism." Yet, while Islamic terrorism is a fact, our government refuses to acknowledge that it is Islam that has declared war against the West. Islam is a "religion of peace," it repeats over and over again; it is only against its "militants," "radicals," and "extremists" that we must take action against. Islam is not totalitarian, it is merely another religion whose adherents must not be offended or provoked. We have only to fear its foot soldiers, the terrorists. Once we have captured, neutralized, or killed them, we can live in peace.

But Islam has an inexhaustible pool of Muslims willing to die as "martyrs." Western leaders and intellectuals refuse to consider the source: Islam itself. So the "war on terror" will continue indefinitely, wasting lives, treasure, and time, until the U.S. is ground down by an enemy dedicated to conquest and victory....

We now have had a succession of Commanders-in-Chief and an emasculated military dedicated to defending this country against its enemies by adopting a policy of not identifying either the enemy or a rational reason for fighting him....

With few exceptions, our politicians and mainstream intellectuals do not grasp the essence of Islam, and do not have the moral rectitude to defend America. Our enemy, however, does know, and does have a blood-thirsty desire to achieve its goals – which is world-wide poverty, slavery, and destruction. To quote from the Brotherhood's 1991 *Explanatory Memorandum: A General Strategic Goal for the Group in North America*:

> The process of settlement is a "Civilization-Jihadist Process" with all the word means. The Ikhwan [the Brothers] must understand that their work in America is a kind of grand Jihad in eliminating and destroying the Western civilization from within and "sabotaging" its miserable house by their hands and the hands of the

believers so that it is eliminated and God's religion is
made victorious over all other religions.

Our country is indeed self-destructing in the "miserable" hands of its
quavering, irrational, evasive, and morally rudderless policymakers. In
contrast, Islam has never been afraid of using the term "victory," and
hasn't the least inhibition in imposing its "cultural values" on the rest of
the world....

Islam has been nothing but consistent, from its very beginnings in the
7th century up through the 21st. The West, and especially the U.S., to
avoid being called "extremist" or "Islamophobic," has consistently
responded with a patchwork of pragmatic policies that eschew any kind
of consistent, principled stand against a committed enemy, policies
which evade identifying the enemy and which have surrendered ground
to the terrorists and their sponsors on virtually every occasion. And on
every occasion, such policies have backfired – as in Afghanistan, Egypt
and Libya – and only emboldened Islamic terrorists and their sponsors.

Source: *Islam's Reign of Terror,* pp. 42-46

☪

The More Things Change....

...the more they stay the same.

Islamic pirates seize commercial vessels off or near the coast of Somalia and hold them and their crews and passengers for ransom. Iran seizes commercial vessels in the Persian Gulf and the Straits of Hormuz and holds them for political ransom and political extortion.

The Rio Norte Line site features an excellent recounting of Thomas Jefferson's experiences with the Islamic jihadists of his day, and how he proposed to deal with the looters. The following is an excerpt from that site.

In March 1785, Thomas Jefferson and John Adams went to London to negotiate with Tripoli's envoy, Ambassador Sidi Haji Abdrahaman (or Sidi Haji Abdul Rahman Adja).

When they enquired "concerning the ground of the pretensions to make war upon nations who had done them no injury," the ambassador replied:

> It was written in their Koran, that all nations which had not acknowledged the Prophet were sinners, whom it was the right and duty of the faithful to plunder and enslave; and that every Musselman who was slain in this warfare was sure to go to paradise.

> He said, also, that the man who was the first to board a vessel had one slave over and above his share, and that when they sprang to the deck of an enemy's ship, every sailor held a dagger in each hand and a third in his mouth; which usually struck such terror into the foe that they cried out for quarter at once.

Thomas Jefferson, in preparation for negotiations with the Tripoli's Ambassador, obtained a Koran in the original language. (Perhaps the same Koran Obama uses at Iftar Dinners held in America's Whitehouse.) Jefferson then taught himself yet another language and reviewed the Koran. Jefferson concluded (rightly as history shows) from his studies and negotiations with the Ambassador that FORCE was the only way to stop the predations of the Muslim states upon America. [Or, retaliatory force against the initiation of force.]

In history are lessons already learned that we may review for guidance in our "modern age." If a People is made purposely ignorant, they are subject to fear, domination, and control."

Barbary corsairs and crews from the North African Ottoman provinces of Algiers, Tunis, Tripoli and the independent Sultanate of Morocco under the Alaouite Dynasty (the Barbary Coast) were the scourge of the Mediterranean. Capturing merchant ships and enslaving or ransoming their crews provided the Muslim rulers of these nations with wealth and naval power. The Roman Catholic Trinitarian Order or Order of "Mathurins" had operated from France for centuries with the special mission of collecting and disbursing funds for the relief and ransom of prisoners of Mediterranean pirates. According to Robert Davis, between 1 million and 1.25 million Europeans were captured by Barbary pirates and sold as slaves between the 16th and 19th centuries.

Barbary corsairs led attacks upon American merchant shipping in an attempt to extort ransom for the lives of captured sailors, and ultimately tribute from the United States to avoid further attacks, much like their standard operating procedure with the various European states.[4] Before the Treaty of Paris, which formalized the United States' independence from Great Britain, U.S. shipping was protected by France during the Revolutionary years under the Treaty of Alliance (1778–83). Although the treaty does not mention the Barbary States in name, it refers to common enemies between both the U.S. and France, which would include the Barbary States or pirates in general. As such, piracy against U.S. shipping only began to occur after the end of the

American Revolution, when the U.S. government lost its protection under the Treaty of Alliance.

Source: "Thomas Jefferson, 1785, reports Ambassador's explanation for making war upon America"
http://therionorteline.com/2014/10/07/thomas-jefferson-1785-reports-ambassadors-explanation-for-making-war-upon-america/

Defending Freedom of Speech

Property rights are essential to guarantee freedom of speech. Without property rights, there can be no freedom of speech, wrote Ayn Rand, the novelist/philosopher. On the inauguration of President John F. Kenney's "Fascist New Frontier," she wrote in another pamphlet:

> "Freedom of speech means freedom from interference, suppression or punitive action by the government – and nothing else. It does not mean the right to demand the financial support or the material means to express your views at the expense of other men who may not wish to support you. Freedom of speech includes the freedom not to agree, not to listen and not to support one's own antagonists. A "right" does not include the material implementation of that right by other men; it includes only the freedom to earn that implementation by one's own effort. Private citizens cannot use physical force or coercion; they cannot *censor* or *suppress* anyone's views or publications. Only the government can do so. And *censorship* is a concept that pertains *only* to governmental action."

The initiation of force by Islamic terrorists to suppress or censor the visual depiction of Mohammad and in serious or satirical literary works is obvious. What some critics of Pamela Geller are now advocating, posing as "defenders of freedom of speech," is a blanket prohibition on art or literary works that may *provoke* terrorists into initiating force. This thoroughly disgusting and craven submission to Islam has the *tacit* approval of our government. By implication, this is also a tacit sanction by those critics and the government of the terrorists to censor by violence any statement the terrorists wish to suppress or punish.

Geert Wilders, the Dutch parliamentarian who has for years been the outstanding champion of freedom of speech in Europe and the object of Islamic and government enmity, and on whose head is a continuing death fatwa, was a featured speaker at the Draw Mohammad event in

Garland, Texas. The Gatestone Institute has printed a version of a speech on freedom of speech and the importance of the First Amendment that he has given elsewhere.

Freedom of speech is under threat today. Not only in Europe, where I come from. But also here, in America.

The last time I was in the United States was less than two weeks ago. I was in Garland, Texas, where I gave the keynote speech at a contest of Muhammad cartoons.

The contest was held in a conference center, where after the Paris *Charlie Hebdo* assassinations, an Islamic organization had convened to demand that freedom of speech be restricted and Muhammad cartoons be forbidden. The Muhammad cartoon contest in Garland was organized to make a stand against this demand. We should never allow ourselves to be intimidated.

The winner of the Garland contest was a former Muslim. There was something very symbolic about the fact that he was an apostate. Under Islamic Sharia law, apostasy is punishable by death. Under the same law, making illustrations of the prophet Muhammad is also punishable by death.
The winner of the contest had made a picture of a fierce looking Muhammad, waving a sword. "You cannot draw me," Muhammad said. Underneath the picture, the artist had written: "That is exactly why I am drawing you!"

That is the true American spirit. This cartoonist is an example to us all.

Under Islamic Sharia law, depicting Muhammad is a crime. But as an American, the artist is not living in an Islamic country. He is living in America. And here, in America, you are allowed to make pictures and drawings, no matter what the Sharia says. And you are also allowed to change your religion and become an apostate. And we should allow no one ever to rob us of these freedoms. If America were to give in to Islamic law, it would no longer be America. Its Judeo-Christian values would be lost. Its civilization would be lost. Its freedoms would be lost.

The enemies of our civilization try to impose Sharia law on us. Barely a few minutes after I had given my speech in Garland, two jihadis attacked the event. They shot a police officer in the leg, but fortunately they were killed before they could do more harm. Through violence and terrorism, these two jihadis tried to impose Sharia law on America. Thanks to brave American policemen, they did not succeed.

We should never allow the terrorists to win. If we react to threats over cartoons by no longer making cartoons, the terrorists have won. But if we react by drawing and showing even more cartoons, the signal is clear: Terror has no effect on us. We will not be intimidated by terror and violence, by doing exactly the opposite of what terrorists want. The terrorist will have lost.

This is why I have invited the Garland Mohammed cartoon exhibition to be shown in the Parliament of the Netherlands. We should show it all over the free world. In Europe and America, Canada, Australia, in the entire free West -- we have to stand up for freedom and make a stand against Islam.

Before I continue, allow me to tell you a little bit about myself.

I am an elected politician, a member of the House of Representatives in the Netherlands. I am the leader of the Party for Freedom. In the last general elections, we gained about 10% of the national vote. I speak on behalf of almost 1 million people. My party is not a marginal phenomenon. It is even the biggest party in a recent major national television poll.

45

However, I have been marked for death. I am on the death list of Al-Qaeda and other Islamic organizations, such as the Pakistani Taliban, and ISIS. For over ten years now, I have been living under 24/7 police protection. I have lived with my wife in army barracks, prison cells and safe houses, just to be safe. Wherever I go, armed policemen accompany me to protect me.

The jihadis want to kill me, but others want to silence me. Not by murdering me, but by legal or political harassment. They try to convict me in court or have me banned. All this is happening not in third-world dictatorships, as you might expect, but in Western democracies.

In my country, the Netherlands, I had to stand in court a few years ago because I spoke out against Islam and the Islamization of my country. Fortunately, I was acquitted. But now I have been charged again. And the only reason is that I have voiced my opinion. They call my speech "hate speech," but I do nothing else other than defending the Judeo-Christian values of our civilization and speaking the truth about Islam.

Two months ago, I was in Austria, where I spoke in the Hofburg Palace in Vienna about the threat of Islamization in Europe. Islamic organizations demanded that the Austrian authorities prosecute me for my words. And last month, I was in the German city of Dresden, where I addressed 15,000 people at a public rally. The public prosecutor had officers attend the meeting in order to listen to what I said, so that they could assess whether to charge me with incitement.

Is there a spy or a public prosecutor in this room? I don't think so. America does not muzzle people.

Two weeks ago, I was in Washington DC for a meeting with members of your Congress, at the invitation of congressmen who wanted to inform themselves about the situation in Europe. Two Muslim congressmen, Keith Ellison and André Carson, however, wanted to have me muzzled. They tried to have me banned from entering your country. They were unsuccessful. Because in America, people are still free to speak. And I have no doubt, Americans will never give up that freedom.

Because it is the essence of what make America *America*! It is what makes America unique.

There is more at stake than our freedom of speech. Our very existence, our freedom to exist, is in danger. If we allow ourselves to be self-censored about anything we say about Islam, then soon Islam will start to tell us how to live, how to dress, how to breathe.

We will even lose the right to life if we do not follow Sharia's commands. If we give in to totalitarianism, we will lose everything, including our lives. That is how civilizations decay. That is how democracies perish.

It is our duty to ensure that this never happens.

Of course, I realize that while most terrorists today are Muslims, not all Muslims are terrorists. Of course, I realize that the terrorists are only a minority -- but they are many.

Research by the University of Amsterdam showed that 11% of the 1 million Muslims in the Netherlands are prepared to use violence for the sake of Islam. That is 100,000 people in a country of 17 million inhabitants.

The terrorists may be only a minority, but polls suggest that they have the support of the majority.

Surveys in my country revealed that 73% of the Islamic population in the Netherlands consider Muslims who go to Syria to fight in the jihad to be heroes. And 80% of the Turkish youths in the

Netherlands do not think that the violence by groups such as ISIS against non-believers is wrong. Four out of five.

And may I ask: Where are the demonstrations of Muslims who do not agree with the violence committed in the name of Islam and its prophet? I have not seen any of them, have you? The majority may not commit violence, but they do not oppose it either.

We cannot put our heads in the sand and do as if all these facts do not exist. We have to face the reality.

In Nazi Germany, too, it was only a minority that committed the atrocities. But the majority allowed it to happen. In the Soviet Union, too, it was only a minority that committed the horrible crimes. But the majority allowed it to happen.

As Edmund Burke, the great philosopher of liberty, once said: "The only thing necessary for the triumph of evil is for good men to do nothing."

So, this is the first step towards safeguarding our freedoms: Realize the facts, speak out the truth, draw the conclusions, and act upon them. If we do not act, we are bound to lose.

In times like these, when our weak leaders close their eyes to the dangerous threat of totalitarian Islam, in times like these when the task of raising the alarm has fallen on ordinary citizens, in times like these, freedom of speech is more important than ever.

George Orwell once said: "The further a society drifts from truth, the more it will hate those who speak it." That is why your First Amendment is so important. It is needed especially to protect the freedom of speech of those who speak the truth and are hated for it.

The words "hate speech" have a very specific meaning today. Criticizing Islam is considered hate speech nowadays. You are allowed to put a crucifix in a jar of urine. Or depict Israel as a Nazi state. That is not considered an act of hatred. But if you draw a picture of Muhammad or speak out again Islamization or tell the truth about Islam, you are considered to be an extremist, a hatemonger, a provocateur.

The fact is that the more Islam we get, the less free our societies become. During the past decades, our politicians allowed millions of Islamic immigrants to settle within our borders. They came with their culture and with their Sharia law. And now, they try to impose it on us. Instead of saying: 'If you come to our country, you have to adapt to us', our political leaders said: 'Keep your culture, we respect Islam and its sensitivities.' Nowhere the demand was made that the immigrants assimilate.

And now the European nations have fallen so deep that they enforce the Islamic taboos in their own laws. They call it a hate crime when freedom-loving people reject the Islamic taboos. Criticizing Islam has become hate speech, punishable by our own laws.

We are not only confronted with Islamization, but also with the folly of cultural relativism and the weak appeasement mentality of our political leaders. This cowardliness has to stop. If this situation continues to go on, it will lead us straight to catastrophe.

That is why I do what I do. I will not stand idly by and let our civilization and democracy perish. I speak out against Islam and I speak out against our weak leaders. I love my country, I love freedom, I do not want to live in slavery and that is why I speak out.

Without a First Amendment, the consequences for speaking out are harder than if you have a First Amendment. But nevertheless, our duty remains the same: In the name of freedom, we have to speak out. No matter the consequences. Because liberty and dignity, that is what we stand for.

The truth is our only weapon -- we must use it. Free speech is a fragile thing that must be boldly defended. So long as we are free to speak, we can tell people the truth and make them realize what is at stake. The West's political, academic, and media establishment are concealing from the people the true scope of the Islamic threat. We must spread the message. That is our first and most important duty.

If immigrants subscribe to our laws and values, they are welcome to stay and enjoy, as anybody else, all the rights our society guarantees; we will even help them to assimilate. But if they commit crimes, act against our laws, impose Sharia law on us, or wage jihad, we must expel them.

We have to stop pretending that Islam is a religion. Islam is a totalitarian ideology that aims to conquer the West. A free society should not grant freedom to those who want to destroy it. As Abraham Lincoln said: "Those who deny freedom to others, deserve it not for themselves".

Every halal shop, every mosque, every Islamic school, and every burka is regarded by Islam as a step toward the ultimate goal of our submission.

And finally, we must remember that as Islam has global ambitions, we are all in danger. We should stand with every nation and every people who are threatened by jihad. This includes Israel, the only democracy in the Middle East, whose conflict with the Arabs is not about land; it is a conflict between freedom and tyranny. We must all support Israel because we are all Israel. And we should never trust Islamic criminal regimes such as Iran. A treaty with the Islamic State of Iran about nuclear weapons is a travesty and a major threat to the security of Israel and the entire West.

I am from Europe. You are Americans, but we are all in the same boat. We should unite against our common adversary. The Islamic tide is strong, but the West has repulsed it before, and we can do so again.

Ronald Reagan said that "the future does not belong to the fainthearted, it belongs to the brave."

So let us be brave. And secure the future.

This address was delivered in a slightly different form to the Gatestone Institute in New York City, May 12, 2015.

Source: "Defending Freedom of Speech"
http://www.gatestoneinstitute.org/5796/wilders-freedom-of-speech

Postscript

Since the original publication of *Islam's Reign of Terror* by Voltaire Press in 2013, scores of acts of terror have been committed overseas, in the Mideast, and numerous acts committed in the United States, including the Boston Marathon bombing of April 15th, 2013, by two Islamic Chechen brothers. Many would-be domestic Islamic terrorists have been foiled by our hamstrung authorities and arrested. Israel was attacked by Hamas, which was provisionally defeated after the terrorist "government" of Gaza launched thousands of rockets at Israeli population centers. Israel discovered a maze of tunnels emanating from Gaza into Israel, built chiefly with "humanitarian" supplies, such as cement and steel, from Israel and other nations. The tunnel complex was supposed to have enabled Hamas to launch a mass raid on Israel with the purpose of killing thousands of Israelis during a Jewish holiday. Hamas has broken several ceasefires, renewing its rocket attacks.

To be more accurate, nearly 26,000* acts of terror in the name of Islam, have been carried out in the U.S. and worldwide including the ones listed earlier in this pamphlet. These number in the thousands. A Boston jury has found Dzhokhar Tsarnaev, one of the Boston Marathon bombers, guilty and sentenced him to death.

More recently, earlier in 2015, the French satirical magazine, Charlie Hebdo, was attacked by Islamic terrorists for caricaturing Mohammad, and twelve staffers killed. And in Garland, Texas, May 3rd, the Draw Mohammad contest event was attacked, but was foiled by a single policeman, who shot and killed the two gunmen. They were the only "casualties."

Most recently, a new terrorist organization, ISIS, or the Islamic State of Iraq and Syria (or, variously, the Islamic State of Syria and the Levant, or ISL), has emerged and conquered wide swathes of Syria and Iraq. ISIS has killed thousands of Christians, Shi'ites, and members of other religious sects, such as the Yazidis, captured hundreds of non-Sunni women as "sex slaves," and displaced thousands more in its drive to Baghdad to establish a caliphate. ISIS has vowed to carry its terrorism to the U.S. and other Western nations. Western, including U.S., response to the threat has been desultory, at best. Indeed, ISIS is alleged to have been present during the Ferguson, Missouri race riots of August this year. In the meantime, countless Muslim "citizens" of various European countries or residing in the West have traveled to Syria to join the *jihad* against the Syrian and other governments. Their return to Europe and America, armed with new terrorist skills, poses an especially perilous danger.

Finally, the mass, uncontrolled immigration of Mexicans and Central Americans over the U.S.-Mexican border into the U.S. has also enabled the stealth infiltration by *jihadists* into the U.S., posing as Hispanics, from the Mideast and Africa.

* The Religion of Peace, May 19th, 2015 at:
http://www.thereligionofpeace.com/

§ Finis §

Some Recommended Reading:

- Robert Spencer, *Did Muhammad Exist?: An Inquiry into Islam's Obscure Origin.* Intercollegiate Studies Institute, 2012
  - *The Complete Infidel's Guide to the Koran.* Regnery Publishing, 2009

- Steve Emerson, *American Jihad: The Terrorists Living Among Us.* Free Press, 2003
  - *Jihad Incorporated: A Guide to Militant Islam in the Us.* Prometheus Books, 2006

- Melanie Phillips, *Londonistan.* Encounter Books, 2007

- Ayaan Hirsi Ali, *Infidel.* Atria Books, 2008

- Bill Warner, *Sharia Law for Non-Muslims (A Taste of Islam).* CSPI Publishing, 2010

- Geert Wilders, *Marked for Death: Islam's War Against the West and Me.* Regnery Publishing, 2012

- Pamela Geller, *Stop the Islamization of America: A Practical Guide to the Resistance.* WND Books, 2011